All the ghosts in my hometown

Poems by Matthew Borczon

LUCHADOR PRESS

Luchador Press
Big Tuna, Texas

Copyright © Matt Borczone, 2025

First Edition: 1 3 5 7 9 10 8 6 4 2

ISBN: 979-8-89975-013-7

LCCN: 2025938311

Cover image: Jon Lee Grafton

Title page image: Matt Borczon

Author photo: Matt Borczon

Acknowledgments

Special thanks to the publications that first published
these poems:

The following have appeared in the following journals *1028
Peach st., Best poetry online, Stanley, Asylum floor #3, Seth, Asylum
Floor#3, Nancy, Asylum floor#3, Stanley #2, Punk noire magazine,
Chris, punk noire magazine, Alice#3,Chewers, Genghis Khan had
over 200 falcons, misfit magazine, It Was, Rasputin, Stanley JR ,Rusty
Truck, Band Reunion, Rusty Truck, Harry Houdini, Rusty truck.*

Table of Contents

"*All the ghosts in my hometown,* the latest collection by the prolific Matt Borczon is surely aptly titled. To call it a love letter to the poet's hometown or a nostalgic ode to adolescence would adequate only in the most basic of interpretations. Indeed, the collection provides nuanced, multi-faceted analyses of what it means to have lived the life that Borczon has. While for sure there are brief glimpses of sweet reminiscence, the poet drills down and expresses the ambiguous nature of our collective existence. There's something beautifully universal without losing the razor-edged specificity that Borczon is known for. When reaching the final poem of the collection, the reader feels as though they have shared all of these experiences, lived a parallel life with the poet, and that is precisely what makes *All the ghosts in my hometown* so successful, and so deeply moving. Matt Borczon has long-established himself as one of the most engaging poets writing today, but with *All the ghosts in my hometown*, he has once again raised the bar for writers and readers alike."

-James Benger, author of *One Week*

"In his latest collection, *All the Ghosts in My Hometown*, Matt Borczon maps the lives of the tender, lost misfits and dreamers he knew growing up in Erie, Pennsylvania. Borczon's Erie is not the Erie of posh lakeside yacht clubs and wind-sails and boat drinks. The human landscape of Borczon's world is often box-cutter and bullet violent, a place where a sad girl cuts herself and saves her blood in old soda bottles; a place where a sweet stripper believes numerology can help anyone pick their perfect pet and the moon is sinking into the earth so fast she can feel it; a place where a coal miner's memory of light amounts to stars piercing the sky like pinholes on the lid of a coffin. Borczon's people are rendered with a complexity and tenderness that can come only from a writer who's been there, in both that darkness and light, himself. In one poem, the speaker imagines gathering again with his childhood bandmates, and how, after years of loss and experience, "we can/ all plug in/ and play/ Knocking on /Heaven's Door /and mean it / like we never could /at nineteen." This is a beautiful, longing, heart-rich book about growing up and growing old, and the empathy, understanding, and wisdom only age can bring."

-Lori Jakiela, author of *All Skate: True Tales from Middle Life*

"While the rest of use are still fumbling with words, Matt Borczon has been writing his poems with flamethrowers, showing what war does to soldiers when they come home. In *All the ghosts in my hometown*, he turns his vision to the things closet to us all, our neighborhoods, and he shows us how those things haunt our days. Here are the guys working factory jobs as they close, and here they are trying to drive a train into the closing factory. These poems are beautiful and terrifying. The daughters of union organizers are here, and they're afraid to get shot because they know the bullet holes and remember their fathers. Coal miners speak like poets. Strippers struggle with stripping. Harry Houdini's escapes are an inspiration. So many of these poems have names as titles. Seth. Becky. Stanley. Jenny. Alice. Stanley, Jr. If you've never looked at yourself and wondered what was wrong, read this book. If you've never looked at your neighbors and wondered what was wrong, read this book. Matt will show you what's wrong with all of us—our insecurities, our violence, our desire for love and our desire to run from love—then remind you that we're together in in this burning ball of water and dirt and that we need to do better, and how dong better is so hard or almost impossible. I read this twice before I wrote this blurb. I'm going to read it again."

-Dave Newman, *Better Than the Best American Poetry*

To Dana Borczon

All the ghosts in
my hometown

Heather

I was
walking
like I
was leaving
town or
trying to
march into
the valley
of death
itself
but all
I was
really doing
was running
away from
heart break
and pain
from a
girl who
left me
the summer
before college
but wouldn't
tell me
until Christmas

so I
just walked
20 miles

in the snow
around the
lake and
finally back
home like
a carrier
pigeon with
a note

that I
was still
not ready
to read.

Stan Quit

high school
in his
senior year
for a
job at
GE building
trains over
the years
he moved
up slowly
until now
50 years
later he
test drives
each locomotive
before they
ship it
over seas

on the
day they
announced the
plant was
closing Stan
drove a
train strait
through the
North gate
fence yelling

like a
cowboy but
the track
ended about
quarter mile
away and
the security
guard found
Stan sitting
at the wheel
crying like
a baby

the guard
kept everyone
back until
they could
get Stan's
wife there
to take
him home.

Last night

Rochelle set
Lumpy's house
on fire
by throwing
her cigarette
onto the
bed after
soaking his
clothes in
gasoline
then she
grabbed his
son from
his first
marriage
and ran
outside

she pulled
the kid
close to
muffle his
cries
but only
so she
could hear
Lumpy scream.

Lizzies

father was
shot dead
on a
street car
for trying
to organize
a union
in the
coal mining
town they
lived in
in the
early forties

the city
left the
hole in
the seat
as a
reminder
of what
happens
when you
don't know
your place
and Lizzie
was afraid
to sit
anywhere

near there
most days

her brothers
would stick
their fingers
in the hole
and swear
they could
still smell
the blood.

1028 Peach st.

In the
neon hour
before sunrise
I am
in a
parking lot
looking at
a fence
that was
once my
old apartment

I spent
almost ten
years above
a paint
store across
from the
YMCA there
were three
roommates
then two
engagements
that were
doomed before
they started

not Romeo
and Juliette

doomed but
more like
Tom and Jerry
Tweety and Sylvester
Itchy and Scratchy
While E coyote
and the road runner

we chased
each other
through our
two bedrooms
with Acme
bought love
while anvils
fell hard
on all
our life
plans

back when
we thought
we knew
what we
were doing

back when
we thought
we had
nothing but
time.

Tuesday

she thinks
numerology
can pick
your perfect
pet and
that the
moon is
slowly sinking
towards earth
from the
sky and
she shoots
pool with
one hand
because her
father lost
an arm
before he
taught her
the game
she thinks
she can
read the
future in
dreams and
she is
certain that
fake tits
won't make

her any
more money

not in
these Pennsylvania
strip clubs
anyway.

David

the day
you died
you gave
me Townes'
broken tooth
the tracks
on Steve
Earls arms
Tom Waits
old piano
and Elliot
Smiths' tears
Chet Bakers
horn and
Hank Williams
Stetson hat
John Prine's
throat cancer
and Merle
Haggard's Prison
sentence

all of
it in
the record
collection I
took out
of your
house on

the same
day we
found more
empty vodka
bottles than
the five
of us
could carry
in one trip.

Stanley

used to
say that
between
3rd shift
and black
lung a
coal miner
is as
dark inside
as out
he said
the first
time you
pick up
your pail
and head
down into
the mine
you sign
your death
warrant
and after
that the
only light
you ever
see is
the stars
in the
sky before

sunrise
like tiny
pin holes
in the
lid of
your coffin.

Becky

It was
hard to
watch Becky
strip in
the club
I worked
in after
college
we had
played together
as kids
and her
brother was
in my
class all
through school
so watching
her dance
naked made
me uncomfortable

almost as
uncomfortable
as I
felt when
she stopped
me to
ask if

I would
please not
say anything
to her
mother when
I saw
her at
church on
Sunday.

August 16 1977

the day
Elvis Presley
died
I was
11 and
had walked
to see
a karate
school where
the teacher
had a
fancy gold
uniform and
the sign
on the
door said
home of
champions
but as
I walked
up to
look in
the window
I stood
by a
newspaper box
with the
headline the
king is dead

and I
stood there
instead
reading the
story over
and over
thinking about
his music
and movies
on Saturday
afternoon TV
about my
father loving
him and
hating the
Beatles
and I
never went
into the
karate dojo
because even
then I
knew champions
come and
champions go
but there
is only
one king.

The girl with the Russian name

As rain
falls on
windshields
chem trails
cross blue
black skies
the color
of ink
on a
Sumi brush
the young
girl with
the Russian
name is
slowly filling
a soda
bottle with
her own
blood she
will soon
tape it
closed and
label it
with the
name of
who she
blames for
her pain
under her

bed is
one that
says mom
and another
that says
life she
hides them
carefully
like the
scars she
has on
her inner
thighs.

Seth

They found
him in
his grandma's
basement
after he
stabbed
that boy
with a
box cutter
after shop
class the
blade was
just long
enough to
nick his
aorta and
the blood
ran as
the color
drained
from his
face I
slipped
in it
as I
watched
that kid
fall down

later
Seth would
say he
was bullied
say it
was over
a girl
say it
was voices
in his
head say
all the
things you
say when
you can't
figure out
how to
say you
have finally
had
enough.

Lydia

She played
drums in
marching band
all through
high school
laughed at
and called
names she
felt invisible
and small
so when
we met
in college
she was
determined
to re-invent
herself and
when she
sat in
with my
band I
was excited
we sounded
better and
my dreams
started to
pinwheel
out of
college bars

and on
to the
road and
success
living
like a
rock star

when she
started
to miss
practice I
called her
house and
her brother
said she
had run
off with
a guy
she had
only just
met her
parents
were frantic
police contacted

and I
couldn't even
be mad
I knew

she was
looking for
a new
life a
fresh start
the cosmic
do over
and when
it came

she took
it like
a rock star.

Nancy

I was
in a
college
poetry class
trying to
write the
academic poem
about your
fight with
leukemia

it was
something
about folding
paper cranes
while you
were in
a blue
turban lying
in a
hospital bed
wondering if
you were
too tired
to go on

I was
trying to
take directions
from the
professor
and my
classmates
about form
and rhythm

but all
the while
I remember
thinking that
all I
really
wanted to
do was
write the
word no
1000 times

over and
over again
until you
were gone.

Stanley #2

My grandfather
used to
say that
when you
die you
are re-
incarnated
on another
planet and
we used
to laugh
at this
idea until
years later
when I
read that
physicists
have the
same theory
provable by
math
and now
I think
that maybe
the universe
is not
so complicated

maybe all
you need
to understand
it is
two fingers
of bourbon
after a
third shift
at the
paper factory.

Chris

You were
drunk enough
to let
me drive
your car
and I
was drunk
enough to
try even
though I
didn't have
a license
and we
zig -zagged
the dirt
roads around
Edinboro lake
that night
past the
summer cottages
like we
had nothing
to lose
or look
forward to

you were
an English
major who

would end
up working
in computer
sales with
Parkinson's
writing songs
no one
would ever
sing and
I was an
Art major
who would
wrap the
stumps of
soldiers in
Afghanistan
but on
that night
we were
just two
drunk college
idiots who
didn't care
if we
lived or
died back
before life
showed us
it didn't
matter anyway

Pretty easy

She had
black finger
nail polish
and hated
my poetry
wore tight
crop top
tee shirts
and got
all the
attention
from the
older boys

until that
night high
and depressed
she decided
she was
being ignored
and jumped
off the
second floor
balcony
landing in
a bush
that cut
her face
up bad
and forever

after that
she really
was ignored
and finally
had to
realize that
the older
boys never
found her
fascinating
only pretty
and easy
like the
nickname they
called her
when she
wasn't around.

First love

at 15
I had
long hair
and wore
an Army
surplus store
jacket as
I walked
to my
girls house
she lived
on South Shore
in a
neighborhood
so rich
you would
drive through
it at
Christmas like
it was
another present
so rich
the police
used to
pick me
up nightly
as I
walked home

over time
they got
used to
me and
said it
was only
because
they got
3-5 calls
a night
about me
from the
residents
that they
still came

to get
me said
they were
sorry and
they knew
I was
not dangerous

this was
about the
time my
girl figured
out I
wasn't dangerous
either so

she left
me for
a guy
who was
and
who made
her father
angrier than
me.

Dumbass kids

The night
some guy
pulled a
gun on
us at
the bar
we worked
in he
put the
barrel against
Mikes Forehead
and I
was talking
fast as
a race-car
and pinning
mikes arms
to his
sides so
he wouldn't
get his
head splattered
across the
cigarette machine

I finally
talked the
guy outside
where he

kept waving
his gun
around until
the cops
arrived
then Mike
and I
drank until
the sun
came up
but we
were still
sober when
the owner
came in
to open
the bar.

Jennie

once told
me that
her oldest
son tried
to kill
her with
a hammer
that he
is mentally
ill and
will be
locked up
probably
for the
rest of
his life

her other
kids are
mad that
she still
takes his
phone calls
from prison
so she
lets him
call her
at work
where I

hear her
in the
break room
promising
that she
will do
what ever
it takes
to get
him out
of there

choking back
tears she
tries to
sound like
she means
it.

Alice#3

the only
time Alice was
ever really
angry with
me was the
day I
stopped over
to tell her
how sorry
I was
to hear
that Betty
had passed
away in
the nursing
home

Betty was
Alice's neighbor
and best
friend and
most likely
more than
that since
the house
she lived
in for
fifty years
also belonged
to Alice

on that day
Alice had
red eyes
and snapped
at me like
a pit bull

be sorry
she was
suffering
don't be
sorry she
is gone

then she
looked at
me like
she wanted
to hit me
or cry.

Genghis Khan had
over 200 falcons

He was
dyed blonde
and lived
on a diet
of steroids
and protein
powder he
tended bar
at the place
I worked
he used
to tell
everyone
he had
slept with
over 100
girls and
when I
asked
him if
any of
these women
ever slept
with him
twice
he looked
at me
with eyes

that said
he didn't
know and
didn't care.

It Was

a story
I heard
many times
both from
Sherrie and
from Dottie
her mom

how one time
in a department store
Dottie was
really wanting
 this beautiful
 oak cabinet
 but told her
kids she wanted
but did not
need it
when Sherrie
says mom
we have
all the things
we need
but none
of the things
we want
so Dottie
bought it
with the

child support
check they
only sometimes
got in
the mail

Sherrie died
about ten
years later
of an
overdose
proof that
she was
always more
interested
in what
she wanted
than what
she needed

and Dottie
died at 80
of old age
and a
broken heart
I don't know
which of
her kids
got that
cabinet when
they cleaned
out her house.

Stanley JR

was 14
and skipping
school the
day some
crazy lady
took 3
shots at
him with
a hunting
pistol on
west 8th
street he
dove behind
a tree
and was
there for
25 minutes
until the
police rushed
her third
floor apartment
and she
put the
gun in
her mouth
and took
the shot
she could
not miss

and Stanley
went home
and never
said a
word to
anyone about
it and
now 42
years later
he eats
amphetamines'
like M and M's
has been
divorced 3
times and
shows up
uninvited to
his daughters
job at
the Mall
like the
ghost of
Christmas yet
to come
he has
a new
woman in
his bed
usually before
the last
one has
gone and

he can
write a
poem that
can make
a grown
man cry
and he
still says
he never
wants to
own more
than he
can fit
into the
backseat of
his car
and I
think that
he is
like this
because
he was
20 years
too young
when he
learned that
time is
an illusion
and nothing
last forever
so he
has spent

his whole
life running
as hard
as he
possibly can
with no
idea where
he was
supposed
to go
because nobody
is ready
to be
that grown
up at
14.

I guess she used
to be a big deal

Coming out
of high school
she was
the head
cheerleader
and went
to a private
college to
be a nurse

but I
did not
remember her
the day
she asked
me maybe
it was
just because
we ran
in different
circles or
maybe it
had been
ten long
years since
we graduated

but she
seemed really
disappointed
I did
not know
her that
day she
came
to the
community
center I
worked in

just before
she checked
all the kids
I worked
with for
lice.

Billy

five kids
age 9
to 13
found the
dead bum
in the
weeds behind
the church
and only
Billy was
upset that
his eyes
were closed

Billy said
I want
to look
for the
the last
thing he
ever saw.

Band reunion

I will
bring the
ghosts from
the last
war you guys
bring the
divorces
and grown
children
the lesbian
affairs and
Brent can
bring the
ashes of
his dead
ex-wife
and we
can all
plug in
and play
Knocking
on Heavens
Door and
mean it
like we
never could
at nineteen

Harry Houdini

once escaped
from the
belly of
an octopus
he was
the first
to fly
a plane
over Australia
and would
escape from
any box
or strait jacket
hand cuffs
or cage
sight unseen

so when
I was
sixteen
shy and
unable to
fit in
too small
for football
and bullied
for my
long hair
and unpopular

taste in music
I carried
his biography
with me
daily like
a bible

proof you
could escape
anything
if you
really really
tried.

Matthew Borczon is a poet and artist and retired Navy sailor from Erie Pennsylvania. He has written 18 books of poetry as well as a collection of short stories. Recent titles are *Twelve Gauge* from Rust Belt Press and *Post Deployment* from Dumpster Fire Press. Matt publishes widely in the small press and has been nominated for the Pushcart and best of the Net. He is currently a nurse in a Plasma Donation Center when he is not writing. He is married with four children.

This project was made possible, in part, by generous support from the Osage Arts Community.

Osage Arts Community provides temporary time, space and support for the creation of new artistic works in a retreat format, serving creative people of all kinds — visual artists, composers, poets, fiction and nonfiction writers. Located on a 152-acre farm in an isolated rural mountainside setting in Central Missouri and bordered by ¾ of a mile of the Gasconade River, OAC provides residencies to those working alone, as well as welcoming collaborative teams, offering living space and workspace in a country environment to emerging and mid-career artists. For more information, visit us at www.osageac.org

Osage Arts Community